The
Toi

by Joseph Gelfer

SUMMERSDALE

Summersdale Publishers Ltd
46 West Street
Chichester
West Sussex
PO19 1RP
UK

www.summersdale.com

ISBN 184024 260 4

Printed and bound in Denmark
by Nørhaven Paperback A/S

Contents

In the University Toilets

God is dead –
Nietzsche.
Nietzsche is dead –
God.

I love cats – they taste like chicken.

On the Science Department toilet paper dispenser:

Pull here for Arts degrees.

On the Arts Department toilet paper dispenser:

Pull here for Science degrees.

In the Computer Science Department:

Log on to the network.

In the Middle Eastern Studies Department:

Hussein I'm a liar?

In the Theology Department:

Lord, I prostate myself before you.

In the Medical Department:

Osteoporosis Drama Club – break a leg!

In the Modern Languages Department:

mi cubicle es su cubicle.

In the Classics Department:

**Veni, Vidi, Velcro.
I came, I saw,
I got stuck.**

Why can't we just
all get a bong?

Why don't mathematicians get constipated? Because they can work hard things out with a pencil.

Scratched on the hand-dryer:

Push for a message from your member of parliament.

Due to brain fog all thoughts have been grounded.

Your mission, should you choose to accept it ...

Shouldn't it be spelt 'fonectic'?

At the bottom of the cubicle door:

Beware of
limbo dancers.

I don't want to work but I'm bored of GMTV!

What's the difference between a dead dog on the road and a dead lawyer on the road? There are no skid marks in front of the lawyer.

It's an all-turd state of reality.

Where are all the bisexual lesbians who want to sleep with me?

Why do they call it a building when it's already built?

They paint the walls to cover my pen, but the toilet poet strikes again!

Convincing yourself that a bad idea is a good idea is a bad idea.

**Sex is great!
Beer is fine!
We're the class of '99.**

I think, therefore
I'm single.

Bi British.

It's not premarital sex if you don't plan on getting married.

Blessed are the meek for we shall inherit the earth – if that's alright with you?

**668, the neighbour
of the beast.**

**Free the bound
periodicals!**

Don't hate me because
I'm beautiful – hate me
because your boyfriend
thinks so.

Bad spellers untie!

**Wipe on, wipe off
– Mr Miyagi.**

Time is the enemy –
thyme is merely tasty
with a roast.

Please refrain from clapping between movements and do remain seated throughout the performance.

Tolkien is hobbit forming.

Why is it hard for women to find men that are sensitive, caring and good-looking? Because those men already have boyfriends.

Don't give in to the authorities. Hold on!

Nothing sucks seeds like success.

Fight for the rights of Pansexuals!
What? Shag guys with hooves and flutes?

I came to university to get drunk and shag and I'm almost out of beer.

The speed of time is an astonishing one second per second.

Celebrate Female
Armpit-hair Week.

Apathy rul ...

It is holy and devout
to write graffiti in
the grout.

A closed mind
is a wonderful
thing to lose.

**Times flies
like the wind.
Fruit flies
like apples.**

My mother is a travel agent for Guilt Trips.

Picard and Riker were here.

You are unique – just like everybody else.

**Puns are bad
– poetry is verse.**

I am at one
with my duality.

Question authority!
Why?

Poke smot, man.

Don't hate yourself in the morning – get up after noon!

Cheeses is Lord.

If there was an invisible cat on a chair, the chair would appear empty. The chair already appears empty therefore there is an invisible cat on it.

The X-Piles:
unwanted visitors
from Uranus.

At the Train Station

When I die I want to go peacefully, in my sleep, like my Granddad. Not screaming like the passengers in his Cortina.

Change is inevitable,
except from this
vending machine.

These chocolate bars
taste like cotton.

**Remember – if you
took a crap,
put it back!**

I may be fat,
but you're ugly
and I can go on a diet.

**The Man With The Golden Pun
– shaken, not turd.**

More waste, less flush.

Make Lego, not war!

**Armitage Shanks
flushed away
a fortune!**

**Harry Squatter
and the
Philosopher's Stone.**

If voting could change anything it would be illegal.

Please tell your trousers it's not polite to point. *Please tell your member it's not polite to stare!*

I feel so strongly about toilet graffiti that I signed a partition.

Let the train take the strain.

Become a skinhead before your Granddad does.

Beware of the squitter-bug.

The Ladies Room:

Where no man has gone before.

I hope your life is like this toilet paper – long and useful!

Please do not bite the woodwork when straining.

In days of old when knights were bold and loos were not invented, they'd lay their load down on the ground and walk away contented.

**It's been beautiful,
but I have to YELL NOW!**

**Why do kamikaze
pilots wear helmets?**

Hells bells,
this place smells.

This too shall pass.

If the best things in life are free, how come this just cost me 20p?

This strain will
be departing any
minute now.

S.W.A.L.P. Sealed with a loving piss.

Jesus saves! But Lineker scores on the rebound!

When was the last time this wall was cleaned? 1992?

Turtles crossing …

Oops, I did it again.

There is a fine line between fishing and standing on the shore acting like a nob.

On the contraceptive machine:

Insert baby for refund.

Constipated people don't give a crap.

Follow Through to the Other Side – Jim Morrison.

AT THE TRAIN STATION

Are you thinking
what I'm thinking?

**Guess which bit
I've got pierced?**

Go run and dump!

If you can't beat them, arrange to have them beaten.

I hated flies, until I opened one.

My husband and I have a magical relationship. Whenever I ask him to do something, he disappears.

What's a man's idea of safe sex? A padded headboard.

If I knew you were coming I'd have baked a cake.

I'm not picking my nose – I'm pointing at my brain.

In case of bombing, hide under the urinal – nobody ever manages to hit them.

Stamp out graffiti.

It's just a dump to the left ... and then a dump to the right ...

The central idea is to keep the central idea central.

Stamp collectors should stick together.

In the Workplace

How was my day? What can you say about a day that begins with having to get up?

Working for the boss is
like smoking dope –
the harder you suck,
the higher you get!

**Everything I
need to know I
learnt on remand.**

Most women would rather be cute than intelligent because most men can see better than they can think.

Stressed is only desserts spelt backwards.

A penny saved is nothing really.

The beatings will continue until morale improves.

Change is inevitable – progress is optional.

**Urine the toilet.
Urine trouble.
Look at the mess urine!**

Down U-bend ...

Failure requires
no preparation.

**Consciousness
– the annoying time
between naps.**

**I have not yet started
to procrastinate.**

We must flush out
the undesirables!

I could have been
a contender
– instead I'm here
– just wiping my bum.

If ants drove cars it
would be even harder
to find a parking place.

Stop pulling
my chain!

Will it ever end?

**It's life, but not
as we know it.**

Would you do
that in your
own home?

**Ambition is just
a bad excuse
for not being lazy.**

Thank God for stupid people, for without them the rest of us could not succeed.

Nostalgia isn't what it used to be.

I'm so happy to pee here today.

If I were a Smurf I would have problems here.

Very funny Scotty, now beam my trousers down.

It is better to be
pissed off than
to be pissed on.

I'm not opinionated –
I'm just always right!

All are equal
when seated.

I feel the need to express myself!

I've never seen one like THIS before!

Reality is for people too weak for drugs.

Nobody notices what I do until I don't do it.

I was trying to daydream but my mind kept wandering.

You can fool some of the people all of the time – and those are the people to concentrate on.

Smile, it makes people wonder what you're thinking about.

**If all else fails,
read the instructions.**

The boss loves spiders.

**Friends help you
move house. Good
friends help
you move bodies.**

Only the lead dog gets a change of scenery.

We had no plan
and we stuck
to it well.

**Everyone is
entitled to my opinion.**

**Clean desk
= cluttered drawer.**

Constipate on the
task ahead of you.

Of all the things
I lost, I miss my
mind the most.

Never underestimate
the power of
people in small
groups.

I feel so much better now that I've given up hope.

Rule of thumb: if it has tyres or testicles you're going to have a problem with it.

I got out of bed and made it to the computer – what more do you want?

In the Restaurant

"Employees Must Wash Hands", *I waited and waited, but I finally washed them myself.*

Rats are only star spelt backwards.

100% organic produce.

Choking seriously damages your health.

Grime doesn't pay.

If it wasn't intended to be eaten, why did they shape it like a hotdog?

Love is … not leaving puddles on the floor.

Viva Mullet.

Amoeba here for some time …

Sir! I suggest your motives are totally intestinal!

The Battle of the Bottom – henceforth known as Bidet.

**The toilet is powered
by a 2-stroke floater.**

The Wombles never
really collected
rubbish.

It's more than
my job's worth.

We aim to please
– you aim too please.

McDump – Go Large!

I'll Be Back!

You're too good for him.

Good afternoon Sir, how do you poo?

**Dancing ...
cheek to cheek.**

**Every chap
should have one.**

Evacuation
via rear exit.

Shoot Crusties!

I think the bloke next door is dying.

Close Encounters of the Turd Kind.

My boyfriend said I needed to lose weight. So I dumped him. I reckoned 13 stone was a good start.

It takes the human body only 24 hours to turn good food into crap. It takes this burger bar just 10 minutes.

Behind every
successful woman
there is a
talented cat.

**Better to lose
a lover than
to love a loser.**

**Why do drunk
men miss the toilet?
*Why do sober men?***

Getting on your
feet requires
getting off your arse.

Tall women are admired – short women are desired.

If you sprinkle while you tinkle, do be sweet and wipe the seat.

My mother made
me a lesbian!
*If I give her the wool, will
she make me one too?*

**Children in backseats of
cars cause accidents,
and accidents in the
backseats of cars cause
children.**

**Nuns!
Kick the habit!**

I'm not playing
with myself
– I'm adjusting
my trousers.

Sticks and stones may break my bones but whips and chains excite me.

Don't rub the lamp unless you're ready for the genie.

The best way to a man's heart is to saw his breastplate open.

The more people I meet, the more I like my dog.

Men are like toilets – the good ones are all taken and the rest are full of crap.

Toilet tennis:
Look left, look right,
look left …

**Never trust
a turkey.**

**Jesus saves
Tesco's vouchers.**

Save the whales –
collect the whole set.

Be nice to your children – they get to pick your nursing home.

If you don't want to
wash the dishes,
do them badly
the first time!

This toilet paper is just like Arnold Schwarzenegger – rough, tough and don't take no crap off anybody!

Strangeness is a leg.

At the Pub

Express lane – five beers or less.

No wonder you always go home alone.

On the contraceptive machine:

This chewing gum tastes like rubber.

Campaign for darts at the next Olympics.

**Let's be careful
out there ...**

**The future of the
human race is
in your hand!**

If love is blind why is lingerie so popular?

This pint here tastes like urine.

Blockages in back passages are dangerous.

Beer goggles protect you from unsightly women.

**Stand aside
for the VIP.**

It's rude to share.

I have a real
feeling of deja-poo.

Welcome to Club Latrino.

I'd give my right arm to be ambidextrous.

No matter how good she looks, some other guy is sick of putting up with her crap.

Live each day out as if it were your last ... and one day you will be right.

Beauty is just one light switch away!

The lemmings were pushed!

**Stand closer –
it's shorter
than you think.**

**Life is 5% how what
you make it and 95%
how you take it.**

Be alert!
England needs
more lerts.

**Want a smart blonde?
Get a golden retriever!**

A fool and his money are soon partying.

Don't eat the big mint – it's been tasting a bit sour lately!

AT THE PUB

Don't throw cigarette butts in the urinal – we don't piss in your ashtrays!

Please do not throw matchsticks in the toilets, our crabs have learnt to pole-vault.

Don't throw your cigarette butts in the urinal, as it makes them soggy and hard to light.

Beauty is in the eye of the beer-holder.

Impotence – nature's way of saying 'No hard feelings.'

I shagged your mother! *Go home Dad, you're drunk.*

Don't be sexist
– birds hate it.

**What does loo paper and
the Starship Enterprise
have in common? They
both hang around
Uranus looking for
Klingons.**

**Sometimes I
wake up grumpy –
other mornings
I just let her sleep.**

Jesus saves!
Moses invests!

Necrophillia – the uncontrollable urge to crack open a cold one.

If I complimented your figure would you hold it against me?

Marriage is a
three-ring circus:
engagement ring,
wedding ring,
and SUFFERING!

**Real men don't
read the instructions.**

**We are urinals!
We don't take crap!**

You're only as old as
the woman you feel.

**Health is simply
the slowest way
there is to die.**

**Jacky, I'm
your Dad.**

I married Mrs. Right – then I realised her first name was ALWAYS!

The longest sentence know to man – 'I do.'

No matter how much you shake it, the last drop always falls down your leg.

My wife follows me everywhere. *No I don't!*

By the cubicle floor:

**If you can read this,
you're pissing
on your shoe.**

**My wife and I will
never get divorced –
neither one of us
wants to get lumbered
with the children.**

Try and spot the mystery plopper.

The bigger they are, the harder they fall.

YOU – out of the gene pool now!

Why is it that when a man talks dirty to a woman it's sexual harassment but when a woman talks dirty to a man it's £1.69 per minute?

Captain's Log.

Neighbour's envy – owner's pride.

No one here gets out alive.

**Disappointed?
Too bad.**

**Don't believe
everything
you drink.**

They say all
men are equal
– poor things.

**Remember –
men don't grow up,
they grow bald!**

THE LITTLE BOOK OF

DIRTY JOKES

ED COBHAM

What's long, hard and a bit sh*tty at the end?

One of your jokes.

summersdale *humour*

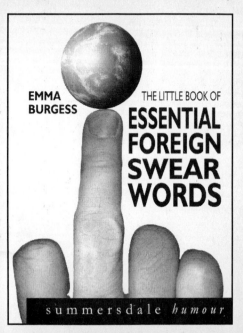

EMMA
BURGESS

THE LITTLE BOOK OF

ESSENTIAL
FOREIGN
SWEAR
WORDS

summersdale *humour*

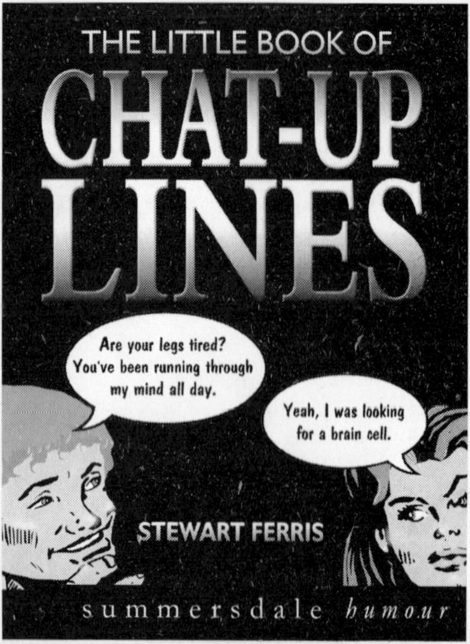
THE LITTLE BOOK OF
CHAT-UP LINES
Are your legs tired? You've been running through my mind all day.
Yeah, I was looking for a brain cell.
STEWART FERRIS
summersdale humour

THE LITTLE BOOK OF

OFFICE
BOLLOCKS

JOSEPH GELFER

summersdale *humour*

For the latest humour books from
Summersdale, check out

www.summersdale.com